Nits!

Written by Zoë Clarke

Illustrated by Maxime Lebrun

RISING ★ STARS

Nick had lots of nits.

Bad luck, Nick!

Nell did not.

Nick had to spray his hair.

Nell did not.

Nick had to wash his hair.

Wash the nits off!

Nell did not.

Nick had to comb his hair.

Pick the nits off!

Nell did not.

Nell has got lots of nits!

Nick has not.

Talk about the story

Ask your child these questions:

1 What did Nick have a lot of?

2 Can you list the three things Nick did to get rid of the nits?

3 Who helped Nick in the bathroom?

4 How did Nell feel about Nick having nits?

5 Have you ever had nits?

6 How do you keep your hair clean and tidy?

Can your child retell the story in their own words?